SUPERCARS

BMW

Christine Webster

AV2
www.av2books.com

AV2

Step 1
Go to **www.av2books.com**

Step 2
Enter this unique code
VPWZXCB0A

Step 3
Explore your interactive eBook!

AV2 is optimized for use on any device

Your interactive eBook comes with...

Contents
Browse a live contents page to easily navigate through resources

Audio
Listen to sections of the book read aloud

Videos
Watch informative video clips

Weblinks
Gain additional information for research

Slideshows
View images and captions

Try This!
Complete activities and hands-on experiments

Key Words
Study vocabulary, and complete a matching word activity

Quizzes
Test your knowledge

Share
Share titles within your Learning Management System (LMS) or Library Circulation System

Citation
Create bibliographical references following the Chicago Manual of Style

This title is part of our AV2 digital subscription

1-Year K–5 Subscription
ISBN 978-1-7911-3320-7

Access hundreds of AV2 titles with our digital subscription.
Sign up for a FREE trial at **www.av2books.com/trial**

SUPERCARS

BMW

CONTENTS

BM

BMW SUPERCARS

A supercar is faster and more expensive than a sports car. Great care is taken when making a supercar. Every detail must be perfect. Most companies will only make a limited number of supercars each year. This is why they can cost hundreds of thousands of dollars.

BMW stands for *Bayerische Motoren Werke*, or Bavarian Engine Work. The company has been on the market for more than 100 years. Today, it is one of the most prominent car makers in the world. It produces cars, including some supercars, and motorcycles.

Only **three BMW Nazca C2s** were ever made.

The BMW **i8** can reach speeds of **155 miles** (250 kilometers) **per hour.**

GUSTAV OTTO AND KARL RAPP

Gustav Otto worked with airplanes. Karl Rapp made different kinds of motors. The two men **merged** their companies during **World War I** to create BMW. In its early years, the company made airplane engines, which were in high demand due to the war.

After the war, German companies had to stop producing parts for war airplanes. BMW decided to start making motorcycles instead. In 1928, BMW bought a car company called Fahrzeugfabrik Eisenach. One year later, the first BMW car was on the market.

Gustav Otto's company was reorganized and renamed Bayerische Flugzeug-Werke in 1916, which is considered the birth year of BMW.

MAP OF GERMANY

BMW's headquarters are located in Munich, Germany. While the company now has more than 30 plants around the world, many important production sites remain in Germany.

THE ROUNDEL

BMW has a distinct, colorful logo, known as the roundel. The logo was first created in 1917. It was composed of a disk, divided into blue and white **quadrants**, surrounded by a black ring with the name "BMW" in white. In 2020, the company unveiled a new logo, in which the black ring was replaced with a transparent one. BMW plans to use the new logo for communication purposes. It has appeared on only one car so far.

The BMW headquarters are shaped like a four-cylinder engine. The BMW logo appears at the top of the building, as well as on the roof of the nearby BMW Museum.

BMW LOGO

The blue and white colors represent the state of Bavaria in Germany. Munich is the capital city of this state.

Some people think that the quadrants represent a spinning airplane propeller.

The round disk with a dark circle was part of the original logo of Karl Rapp's motor company.

BMW THROUGH HISTORY

Otto and Rapp started out in the aircraft industry. Today, BMW is one of the most well-known car brands in the world.

1917

Karl Rapp's company is renamed Bayerische Motoren Werke. BMW keeps this name when Rapp and Otto merge their companies.

1923

BMW introduces its first complete vehicle, the R32 motorcycle.

1951

The company produces the BMW 501, its first car after **World War II.**

BMW creates a company called BMW Motorsport. This new company is in charge of all BMW racing activities.

1972

2013

The i3, BMW's first all-electric vehicle, is launched.

2021

The new BMW iX sport utility vehicle (SUV) is unveiled during the Shanghai International Automobile Industry Exhibition in China.

FAMOUS BMWS

BMWs have appeared in many high-grossing movies. In the Bond movie *GoldenEye*, James Bond swaps his Aston Martin for the BMW Z3.

Different BMW models have made their debuts in other films. Tom Cruise's character drove an i8 in *Mission: Impossible – Ghost Protocol*. BMWs have appeared in other movies in the Mission: Impossible franchise, too.

The original Z3 used in *GoldenEye* is displayed at the James Bond 007 Museum in Nybro, Sweden.

BMWs are also popular offscreen. Many celebrities have used these cars over time. Legendary singer Elvis Presley purchased a BMW during his military service in Germany. Actress Angelina Jolie has been seen riding a BMW Hydrogen 7. National Hockey League player Scottie Upshall used to drive a BMW i8, a **hybrid** supercar.

The *Mission: Impossible – Fallout* movie featured BMW motorcycles.

The Hydrogen 7 was the first commercial vehicle powered by hydrogen.

Elvis Presley owned a BMW 507.

AT THE RACES

The BMW racing team was founded in the 1970s. It competes in several categories, including endurance races, **Grand Touring (GT)**, and Formula E. BMW also has a junior team.

While BMW does not currently race in **Formula 1 (F1)**, it used to take part in F1 races. Race driver Nelson Piquet won the F1 Drivers' World Championship in 1983 with the Brabham BMW BT52.

In recent years, BMW has become involved in **esports**. BMWs are featured in racing simulation video games. The company organizes virtual competitions and supports some of the most successful esports teams.

During his career, Nelson Piquet won three F1 championships.

The Brabham BMW BT52 has an arrow-shaped front wing.

BMW left **F1 racing** in **2009**.

Only single-seater electric race cars can compete in Formula E. BMW currently races in this category with the iFE.21.

The **Brabham BMW BT52** has a maximum **horsepower** of about **1,400**.

Coque López, Nicolás Rubilar, and Randall Haywood raced with the BMW team in the 2020 esports Gran Turismo Championships.

HOW IT'S MADE

BMW plants use some of the most advanced technology in the world, including state-of-the-art **robotics**. Large sheets of metal are stamped out and bent to form the side frames, hood, roof, and doors of a car. These pieces are joined together and sprayed with at least four coats of paint. Then, the car is assembled. The engine is placed inside and started. After many tests, the BMW rolls off the line, ready for its new owner.

The i8 was produced in the BMW plant in Leipzig, Germany. About 20,000 of these cars were made before production stopped in 2020.

BMW has more than 120,000 employees around the world.

BMW has **plants in 15 countries.**

In **2020, BMW** sold more than **2.3 million** vehicles.

The Z3 was the first BMW produced entirely outside Europe. It was made in the Spartanburg plant in South Carolina.

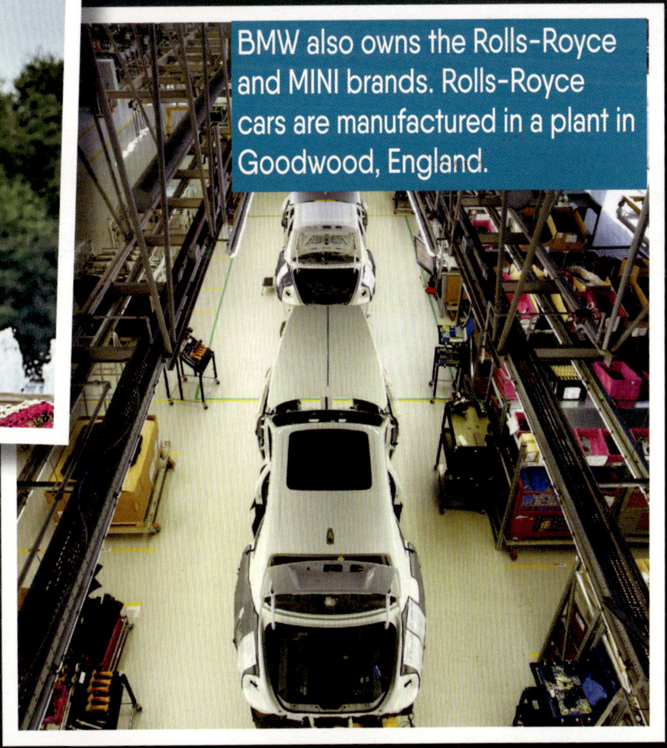

BMW also owns the Rolls-Royce and MINI brands. Rolls-Royce cars are manufactured in a plant in Goodwood, England.

TODAY'S LINEUP

Today's BMWs are modern and elegant cars that meet the needs of drivers. BMW fans can choose between different types of vehicles, including powerful SUVs, such as the X1, and stylish coupes, such as the X6 M Sports Activity Coupe. All models can be customized to make each car unique to its owner.

BMW X1

Engine: **4-cylinder TwinPower Turbo**

Maximum Horsepower: **228**

0–60 mph (0–100 km/h): **6.3 seconds**

Starting Price: **$35,400**

BMW i3s

Engine: **AC Electric Motor**

Maximum Horsepower: **181**

0–60 mph (0–100 km/h): **6.8 seconds**

Starting Price: **$47,650**

BMW Z4 Roadster M40i

Engine: **TwinPower Turbo inline-6**

Maximum Horsepower: **382**

0–60 mph (0–100 km/h): **3.9 seconds**

Starting Price: **$63,700**

BMW M4 Coupe

Engine: **TwinPower Turbo inline-6**

Maximum Horsepower: **473**

0–60 mph (0–100 km/h): **4.1 seconds**

Starting Price: **$71,800**

BMW X6 M Sports Activity Coupe

Engine: **TwinPower Turbo V8**

Maximum Horsepower: **600**

0–60 mph (0–100 km/h): **3.8 seconds**

Starting Price: **$108,600**

BMW M8 Convertible

Engine: **TwinPower Turbo V8**

Maximum Horsepower: **617**

0–60 mph (0–100 km/h): **3.0 seconds**

Starting Price: **$139,500**

TOMORROW'S BMWS

In the near future, BMW will expand its lineup of electric vehicles. The company is expected to launch the i4, a sedan car, and the iX, an SUV, in 2022. These vehicles, equipped with electric engines, will be able to travel more than 300 miles (480 km) between charges.

BMW is also developing cars that will use new technologies, such as **artificial intelligence** and self-driving functions. In the Vision Next 100 **concept car**, a computer called Companion will assist the driver in any situation. Parts of the car will be composed of about 800 moving triangles. These triangles will be able to communicate with the driver and share information about road conditions.

To date the BMW logo launched in 2020 has only been used on the new i4.

Almost all BMW cars, including the iX, have a front grille shaped like a pair of kidneys.

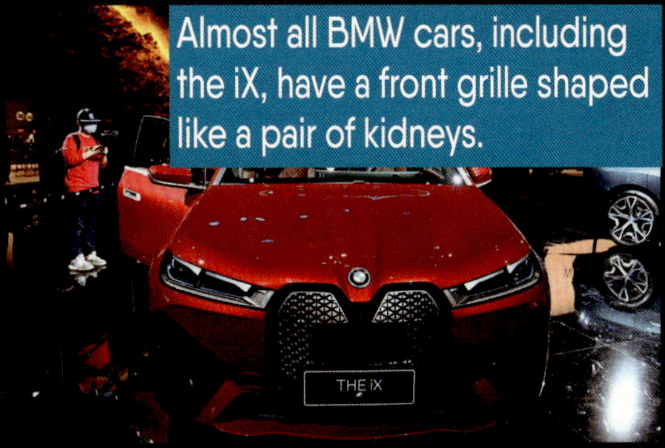

The Vision Next 100 represents the technology BMW intends to develop in the next 100 years.

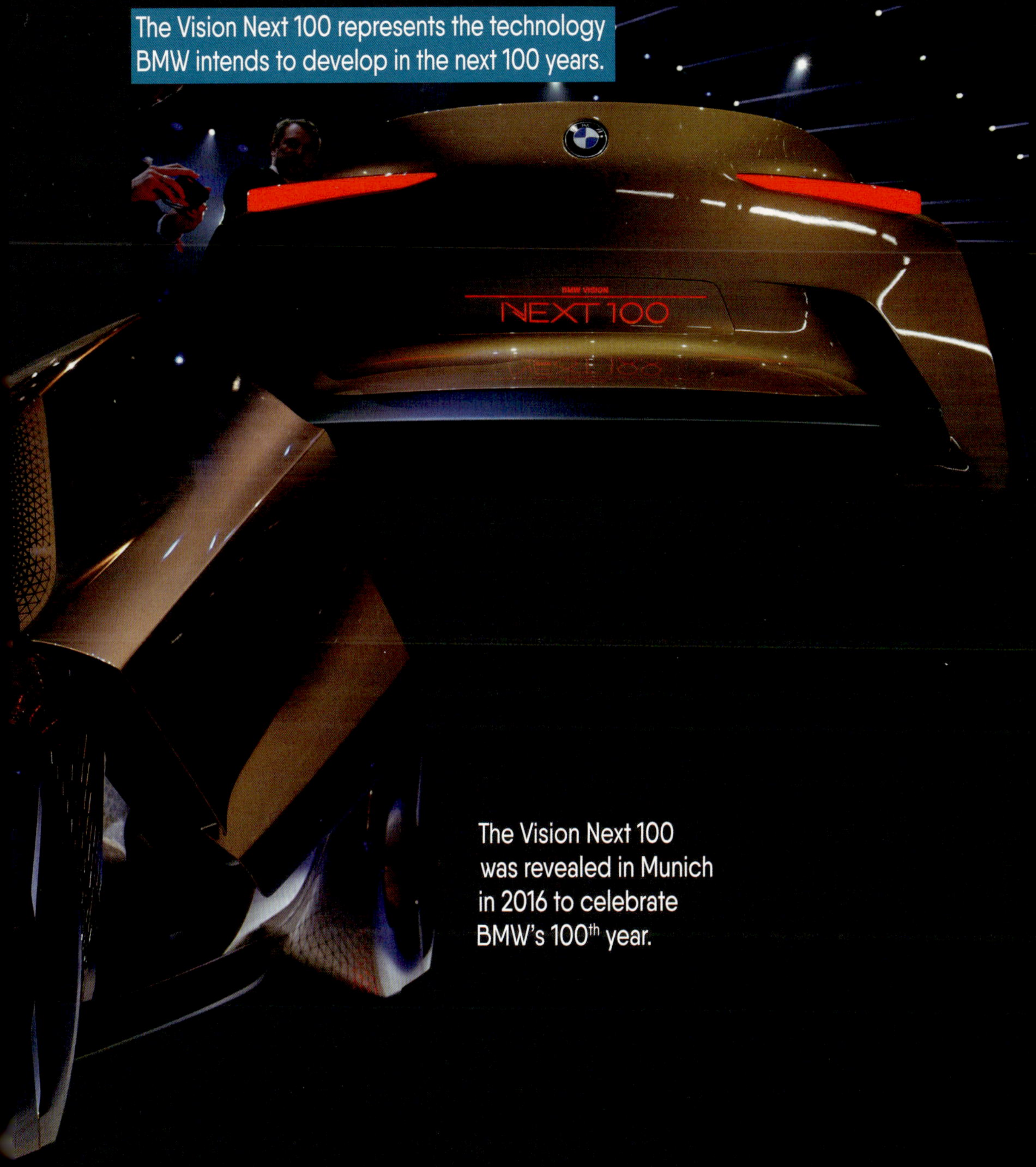

The Vision Next 100 was revealed in Munich in 2016 to celebrate BMW's 100th year.

BMW QUIZ

1 Which year is considered the birth year of BMW?

2 What do the colors of the BMW logo represent?

3 What is the grille on almost all BMW cars shaped like?

4 What is the name of the computer in the Vision Next 100?

5 Where are BMW's headquarters?

6 Who won the 1983 F1 Drivers' Championship?

7 Where was the i8 model produced?

8 How many i8 cars were made before production stopped in 2020?

9 When was the Vision Next 100 revealed?

10 Which was the first BMW car to be produced entirely outside Europe?

ANSWERS

1 1916 **2** The state of Bavaria **3** A pair of kidneys **4** Companion **5** Munich, Germany **6** Nelson Piquet **7** Leipzig, Germany **8** About 20,000 **9** In 2016, to celebrate BMW's 100th year **10** Z3

KEY WORDS

artificial intelligence: the ability of a computer to process information and perform tasks that usually require human intelligence

concept car: a car built to show off new technologies and designs

esports: competitive video games played by professionals

Formula 1 (F1): the highest level of single-seat car racing

Grand Touring (GT): a race car that seats two people

hybrid: powered by both a gas engine and an electric motor

merged: united to create one company

quadrants: four sections of a circle

robotics: use of machines to perform tasks traditionally performed by humans

World War I: a war that was fought mainly in Europe from 1914 to 1918

World War II: a war that was fought from 1939 to 1945

INDEX

Published by AV2
276 5th Avenue, Suite 704 #917
New York, NY 10001
Website: www.av2books.com

Library of Congress Cataloging-in-Publication Data

Names: Webster, Christine, author.
Title: BMW / Christine Webster.
Description: New York, NY : AV2, [2022] | Series: Supercars. | Includes index. | Audience: Grades 2-3.
Identifiers: LCCN 2021022171 (print) | LCCN 2021022172 (ebook) | ISBN 9781791138783 (library binding) | ISBN 9781791138790 (paperback) | ISBN 9781791138806 (ebook other)
Subjects: LCSH: BMW automobiles--Juvenile literature. | Sports car racing--Juvenile literature.
Classification: LCC TL215.B25 W44 2022 (print) | LCC TL215.B25 (ebook) | DDC 629.28/722--dc23
LC record available at https://lccn.loc.gov/2021022171
LC ebook record available at https://lccn.loc.gov/2021022172

Printed in Guangzhou, China
1 2 3 4 5 6 7 8 9 0 25 24 23 22 21

072021
101120

Art Director: Terry Paulhus
Project Coordinator: Sara Cucini

Photo Credits
Every reasonable effort has been made to trace ownership and to obtain permission to reprint copyright material. The publisher would be pleased to have any errors or omissions brought to its attention so that they may be corrected in subsequent printings. AV2 acknowledges Getty Images, Alamy, Shutterstock, and Wikimedia Commons as its primary image suppliers for this title.